Have you ever...

Sounds like a big word! But it just means that a person called a "prophet," has predicted what will happen in the future. Sometimes the prophecy comes true in a day, but sometimes it takes hundreds of years! We've found some really amazing prophecies in the Bible, and we'd love to share them with you! You won't believe some of the things we've found! Come on! Let's check them out together ...

What About Prophecy?

In 1898, a man named Morgan Robertson wrote a book called *The Wreck of the Titan*, which most people thought was just too silly of a story to believe. But 15 years later, a huge ship called *Titanic* proved them wrong! The remarkable parallels between the *Titanic* and the fictional *Titan* seem almost like prophecy ...

	Titan	Titanic
Length:	800 feet	882 feet
Width:	90 feet	92.5 feet
Top Speed:	25 knots	23 knots
Propellers:	3	3
People aboard:	2,000	2,228
Lifeboats:	24	20
Deaths	2,500	2,200

Both ships were struck by icebergs on their right sides and both sank in the month of April! But if you think these similarities are amazing, wait until you hear about the prophecies in the Bible!

Did you know the Bible records at least 1,815 distinct prophecies— spanning more than 8,000 verses? And while most have already come true, many still await their fulfillment at some future point in time. Amazingly, about 425 of these prophecies were fulfilled by the birth, life, death, and resurrection of Jesus.

But why are there prophecies in the Bible in the first place? Well, for one reason, it's one way we know we can trust God and His plan for our lives. "Prophecy never had its origin in the will of man, but men spoke from God as they were carried along by the Holy Spirit" (2 Peter 1:21).

So if you're ever worried about what tomorrow might bring, just pick up your Bible and read about all the fulfilled prophecies like the ones you'll find in this book. Then remember that Jesus has promised amazing wonders for your future. If all the prophecies in the Bible come true, you can know for certain that you'll have an amazing future if you just trust in Jesus!

Vocab Word!

PROPHET: A messenger who has been sent by God.

1 The Very First Prophecy

You might have heard about some of the prophecies in the Bible before picking up this little book. But you can find tons more if you know where to look!

In fact, the very first prophecy in the Bible can be found in Genesis 3:15 ...

God spoke this prophecy with His own lips—and He was speaking directly to the serpent, Satan.

The Prophecy

Genesis 3:15

"I will put enmity between you and the woman. ... He shall bruise your head, and you shall bruise His heel."

God was saying that one day, a child would be born who would be an enemy of Satan. He would even someday destroy the devil forever! Who? That's right: it was Jesus!

Prophecy Fulfillod!

This prophecy was fulfilled by Jesus 4,000 years later ...

... by His birth
Matthew 1:18

... by His death
John 19:30

... by His resurrection
Matthew 28:5,6

The devil tried everything to get Jesus to sin, but it didn't work! He also "bruised" Jesus' "heel" when Jesus was crucified, but Jesus rose from the dead. That was the beginning of the end for Satan.

You might wonder, "When will Jesus finally crush Satan's head?" Read Revelation 20:10!

Vocab Word!

ENMITY: Hostility; hatred; ill will

2 Don't Forget About Jericho

The story of Joshua and the city of Jericho is one of the most popular stories of the Bible. But did you know a prophecy was also given here? Disobeying this prophetic warning came with big trouble, and everyone knew it!

It began when Joshua and the children of Israel, God's people on Earth, witnessed the walls of Jericho fall down. Joshua then gave this prophecy ...

The Prophecy

Joshua 6:26

"At the cost of his firstborn shall he lay its foundation, and at the cost of his youngest son shall he set up its gates."

Joshua was predicting that whoever tried to build Jericho up again would see his oldest and youngest children die!

When?
In 1450 B.C.

This prophecy was fulfilled by a man named Hiel about 530 years later—he lost his sons trying to rebuild the city of Jericho!

Prophecy Fulfilled!

1 Kings 16:34

"In his days Hiel of Bethel built Jericho. He laid its foundation with Abiram his firstborn, and with his youngest son Segub he set up its gates, according to the word of the Lord, which He had spoken through Joshua the son of Nun."

Would you do it? Would you rebuild a city if you knew a curse would be placed on your family? Loving and obeying God is better than disobeying His Word!

Vocab Word!

CONQUER: To be victorious; to gain, or win, or obtain by effort

This incredible prophecy doesn't come from the mouth of a famous man. In fact, we don't even know his name.

Yet God still used him to give a very specific prophecy to His people, the Jews …

The Prophecy

1 Kings 13:2

"Thus says the Lord: Behold, a child Josiah by name, shall be born to the house of David; and on you he shall sacrifice the priests of the high places who burn incense on you, and men's bones shall be burned on you."

This prophet said a boy named Josiah, a great-grandson of King David, would be born and that men's bones would be burned on an altar built by a king named Jeroboam!

When?
In 930 B.C.

Prophecy Fulfilled!

The first fulfillment of this prophecy is found in ...

2 Kings 22:1,2

A boy named Josiah became king at age 8! He was an ancestor of King David.

The second fulfillment of this prophecy is found in ...

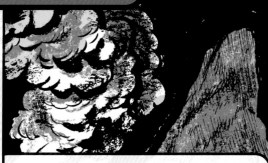

...2 Kings 23:15,16

"He sent and took the bones out of the tombs and burned them on the altar, and defiled it according to the word of the Lord which the man of God proclaimed."

300 YEARS LATER!

These events were predicted 300 years ahead of time! Only the true God could tell a man such details so far in advance.

Vocab Word!

PROCLAIM: To make something known; to declare

Sometimes prophecies cover large periods of time; sometimes it doesn't take long—like only one day!

God's people were at war with three wicked nations at one time. Israel was totally outnumbered and very afraid, but their leader, King Jehoshaphat, had God on his side.

The Prophecy

2 Chronicles 20:17

"You will not need to fight in this battle. Position yourselves, stand still and see the salvation of the Lord, who is with you, O Judah and Jerusalem! Do not fear or be dismayed; tomorrow go out against them, for the Lord is with you."

God's prophet said that all three huge armies would be defeated without Israel doing any fighting at all!

When?
In 850 B.C.

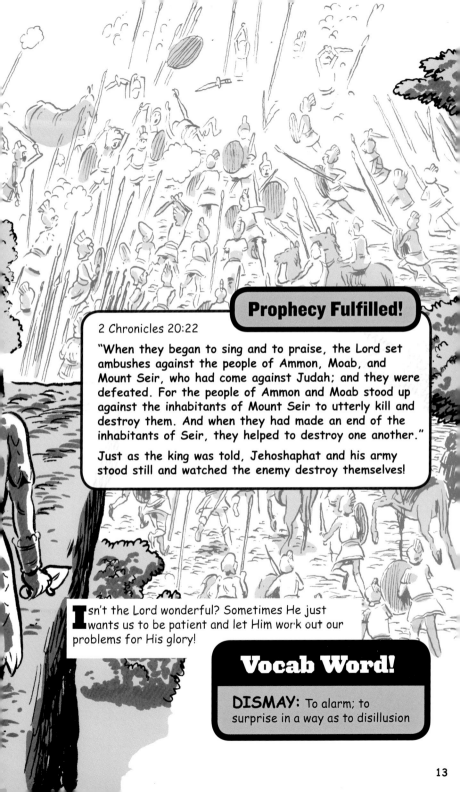

Prophecy Fulfilled!

2 Chronicles 20:22

"When they began to sing and to praise, the Lord set ambushes against the people of Ammon, Moab, and Mount Seir, who had come against Judah; and they were defeated. For the people of Ammon and Moab stood up against the inhabitants of Mount Seir to utterly kill and destroy them. And when they had made an end of the inhabitants of Seir, they helped to destroy one another."

Just as the king was told, Jehoshaphat and his army stood still and watched the enemy destroy themselves!

Isn't the Lord wonderful? Sometimes He just wants us to be patient and let Him work out our problems for His glory!

Vocab Word!

DISMAY: To alarm; to surprise in a way as to disillusion

5 The Desolation of Edom

The land of Edom was a great paradise! It was so beautiful—with everything you could ever want. Everything but God.

Edom was a wicked place, and the people there hated God and often attacked His people. So Jeremiah the prophet said one day, as punishment, Edom would become barren ...

The Prophecy

Jeremiah 49:17

"Edom shall be a horror." A different version of the Bible says, "Edom shall be a desolation."

Each of these words are bad news! The Bible says that people through time would "gasp" in horror at what became of Edom.

When?
In 600 B.C.

Prophecy Fulfilled!

Malachi 1:4

"Edom has said, 'We have been impoverished, but we will return and build the desolate places.'"

Edom was destroyed, yet her people were still defiant. But God didn't change His mind—He wasn't going to let them rebuild!

"Thus says the Lord of hosts: They may build, but I will throw down. They shall be called the Territory of Wickedness."

When God says a place will be barren forever, it will stay that way! To this day, the city of Edom is barren. The old city is gone, and the only thing that remains is the "wall of Petra," a building carved into a mountainside.

Vocab Word!

BARREN: Not producing, unfruitful, dull or empty

If a fortune-teller came on the news and predicted the United States would be destroyed in two years' time, never to rise again—no one would believe him!

But this actually happened hundreds of years ago, when Nineveh, a powerful city, was forever destroyed from the face of the Earth …

When?
In 612 B.C.

The Prophecy

The prophet Nahum predicted …

- The people of Nineveh would be drunk when they were destroyed (Nahum 1:10)

- The commanders of her armies would flee (Nahum 3:17)

- Fire would totally destroy the city (Nahum 3:15)

- The city would never rise again (Nahum 1:14, Nahum 3:19)

Prophecy Fulfilled!

Did you know historical records outside of the Bible often confirm prophecies from God?

All of these predictions against wicked Nineveh came true according to the ancient historian Diodorus Siculus. Pretty amazing, huh?

No matter how strong or mighty a person or nation feels—no one can go against the Word of God and remain standing. That's why you can trust the Lord with your heart and life today!

Vocab Word!

HISTORIAN: A person who studies the history of the world; an expert in history

Imagine your mom telling you, "If you don't clean up your room, a tornado will sweep the whole house away!" You'd probably laugh and laugh at the thought.

But God wasn't laughing when Ezekiel the prophet said every building in a wicked city called Tyre would be destroyed ...

The Prophecy

When?
In 597 B.C.

Ezekiel 26:3

"Thus says the Lord God: Behold, I am against you, O Tyre, and will cause many nations to come up against you, as the sea causes its waves to come up."

That's not all! Get your Bible out and look up the full prophecy in Ezekiel 26:4–6!

Prophecy Fulfilled!

Alexander the Great attacked Tyre in 333 B.C., 250 years later. Tyre was toppled by an invading army, and her buildings were pushed into the sea to build a bridge.

Don't believe it? You can read all about it in your encyclopedia!

Even when God's promises seem totally unbelievable, remember what happened to Tyre! When God makes a promise—it will come true. So when He promises you eternal life in heaven, you can believe it too!

Vocab Word!

TOPPLE: To fall forward, as from having too heavy a top; tumble down

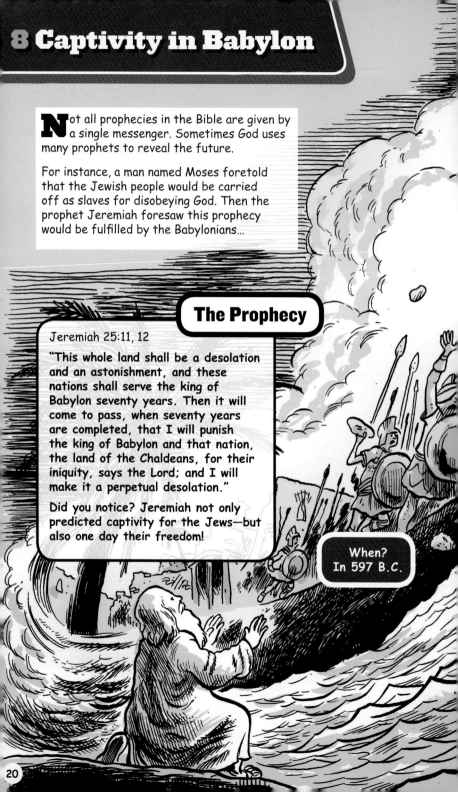

8 Captivity in Babylon

Not all prophecies in the Bible are given by a single messenger. Sometimes God uses many prophets to reveal the future.

For instance, a man named Moses foretold that the Jewish people would be carried off as slaves for disobeying God. Then the prophet Jeremiah foresaw this prophecy would be fulfilled by the Babylonians...

The Prophecy

Jeremiah 25:11, 12

"This whole land shall be a desolation and an astonishment, and these nations shall serve the king of Babylon seventy years. Then it will come to pass, when seventy years are completed, that I will punish the king of Babylon and that nation, the land of the Chaldeans, for their iniquity, says the Lord; and I will make it a perpetual desolation."

Did you notice? Jeremiah not only predicted captivity for the Jews—but also one day their freedom!

When?
In 597 B.C.

Prophecy Fulfilled!

According to history, it took 60 years for this prophecy to come true. Babylon invaded Israel, destroyed their temple, and the Jews were taken as slaves. Yet 70 years after that, the Jews were set free and Babylon was destroyed.

How did that happen? Find out on the next page!

Just as God freed the Jews from Babylon after they turned back to Him, God will forgive and restore you when you say sorry for your sins and turn back to Him!

Vocab Word!

CHALDEAN: An astrologer, soothsayer, or enchanter

Do you know what you would name a son ... if you ever had one? How about the name of your son's son's son? That would be even harder to predict, wouldn't it?

Well, in the Bible, the prophet Isaiah said that a conqueror named Cyrus would destroy Babylon—100 years before Cyrus was even born! He also said this man would conquer the world and free all the Jewish exiles. At the time of this prediction, there weren't any exiles!

The Prophecy

Isaiah 44:28; 45:1

"Who says of Cyrus, 'He is My shepherd. And he shall perform all My pleasure, Saying to Jerusalem, "You shall be built," and to the temple, "Your foundation shall be laid."' ...

Thus says the Lord ... To Cyrus, whose right hand I have held— To subdue nations before him and loose the armor of kings."

Bonus! Look up Isaiah 45:13 for another prophecy about Cyrus freeing the Jewish exiles!

When?
In 690 B.C.

Prophecy Fulfilled!

150 years later, Cyrus was born and began to conquer the world. He let the Jewish people go free in about 540 B.C.

Ezra 6:14 tells us that the Jews rebuilt Jerusalem and finished it according to the commandment of God and according to the decrees of Cyrus, Darius, and Artaxerxes, king of Persia.

Isn't it wonderful that God loves you so much that He promises you can trust Him no matter what happens in this life? Never give up hope—you never know the great things God will do for you just around the corner!

Vocab Word!

SUBDUE: To overcome; to repress; to bring under cultivation

10 The Amazing Statue

The things that happen in the world aren't always easy to understand. Sometimes events happen by surprise—like a natural disaster or the downfall of the nation of Iraq and Saddam Hussein.

Who can know what global events will happen a month from now, much less a decade down the road? Well, the Bible does! Centuries ago, it actually predicted the great empires of world history ...

When?
In 600 B.C.

The Prophecy

Read Daniel 2:31–35

The mighty king of Babylon, Nebuchadnezzar, had a bizarre dream about a giant statue made of gold, silver, bronze, iron, and clay. He didn't understand what it all meant, so he called God's prophet, Daniel, to make sense of it.

Daniel explained that the statue revealed Babylon would one day be subdued—and the nations of Persia, Greece, and Rome would follow.

Prophecy Fulfilled!

Sure enough, over the centuries, God's Word has proven true time and again!

Babylon was conquered by Persia—Persia was conquered by Greece—Greece was conquered by Rome. Just as God said!

Yet the most exciting kingdom to come is represented by the "stone cut without hands." That is a symbol of God's perfect kingdom ruled by Jesus. And it's coming very soon!

You know what this means? Even in strange and troubling times like these, you don't have to worry because God knows everything and He is in control.

Vocab Word!

SYMBOL: A thing that represents or stands for something else

Things around us change so fast! Do you remember the steam engine? How about photographic film? These things were invented less than 150 years ago and changed the world, but they're already outdated today!

Who in Bible times could have ever imagined such a scenario? God's prophet Daniel ... that's who ... more than 2,500 years ago!

The Prophecy

Daniel 12:4

"But you, Daniel, shut up the words, and seal the book until the time of the end; many shall run to and fro, and knowledge shall increase."

This verse talks about the last days—and how knowledge will increase just before Jesus comes again!

When?
In 600 B.C.

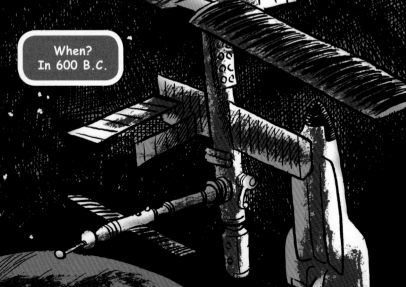

Prophecy Fulfilled!

We see this prophecy being fulfilled every day!

You name it: space stations, superfast computers, smart phones, even the Internet—human knowledge today is exploding.

Can you think of other incredible inventions that show how much knowledge is in the world today?

You might have heard people say we're living in the last days—that the world will end soon. Don't be scared! God saw it coming a long time ago and has a plan to help you survive and thrive!

Vocab Word!

KNOWLEDGE: Information, and skills acquired by a person through experience

12 The Wasteland Babylon

Babylon was a mighty city! 196 miles square and heavily fortified. It had a moat around it and a massive double wall 330 feet high! It also stored enough food to last a whole year in case of an enemy attack.

People thought the city would last forever. God knew better ...

When?
In 690 B.C.

The Prophecy

Isaiah 13:19, 20

"Babylon, the glory of kingdoms, the beauty of the Chaldeans' pride, will be as when God overthrew Sodom and Gomorrah. It will never be inhabited, nor will it be settled from generation to generation: Nor will the Arabian pitch tents there. Nor will the shepherds make their sheepfolds there."

God told His prophets that Babylon would be conquered and never be rebuilt!

Prophecy Fulfilled!

Jeremiah 51:43 talks about Babylon too. "Her cities are a desolation, a dry land and a wilderness, a land where no one dwells, through which no son of man passes."

History records that all this came to pass just as God said it would.

Did you know that a man named Saddam Hussein spent millions of dollars and tried two times to rebuild the city of Babylon? Yet he failed miserably because people can never go against the Word of God and succeed!

Vocab Word!

FORTIFY: To make strong; strength or vigor

13 Jesus' Birth: A Child of Prophecy

Did you know there were prophecies written about Jesus long before He was ever born?

The faithful prophet Isaiah foretold long ago that Jesus would be born of a virgin, and the prophet even told us about His wonderful name! A prophet called Micah even named the town in which Jesus would be born!

When?
In 700 B.C.

The Prophecy

Isaiah 7:14

"Therefore the Lord himself will give you a sign. Behold, the virgin shall conceive and bear a son, and shall call his name Immanuel."

See also Micah 5:2!

Our Savior Jesus was so extraordinary! Fully God and fully human. He also offered us an extraordinary free gift: total freedom from the curse of sin. Jesus died for you; won't you live for Him?

Prophecy Fulfilled!

Matthew 1:21–23

"She will bring forth a Son, and you shall call His name Jesus, for He will save His people from their sins. So all this was done that it might be fulfilled which was spoken by the Lord."

All this came true in the little town of Bethlehem almost 700 years later in about 4 B.C.!

Vocab Word!

EXTRAORDINARY:
Beyond what is usual or regular; exceptional, remarkable, special

14 Jesus Is Betrayed

About 500 years before Jesus' birth, a prophet named Zechariah made a very specific prediction regarding the Savior's final days ...

When?
In 500 B.C.

Zechariah 11:12,13

"'If it is agreeable to you, give me my wages; and if not, refrain.' So they weighed out for my wages thirty pieces of silver. And the Lord said to me, 'Throw it to the potter'—that princely price they set on me. So I took the thirty pieces of silver and threw them into the house of the Lord for the potter."

This says the Messiah would be betrayed for the price of a slave—30 pieces of silver. The money would be used to buy a burial plot.

Psalm 41:9 also says that Jesus would be betrayed by a friend.

The Prophecy

It's comforting to know that even in Jesus' betrayal and death, it did not surprise the Lord—and He also knows what's happening in your life and wants to guide you in the right way!

Prophecy Fulfilled!

Matthew 1:21-23

"Then one of the twelve, whose name was Judas Iscariot, went to the chief priests and said, 'What will you give me if I deliver him over to you?' And they paid him thirty pieces of silver. And from that moment he sought an opportunity to betray him."

This prophecy was fulfilled around A.D. 30.

Vocab Word!

WAGES: Money paid for work

Jesus' death is very important to you and me. It's also one of the most prophesized subjects in the Old Testament.

They were written down hundreds of years before by prophets of God, and each of them came true exactly as predicted.

The Prophecy

Isaiah 53:9–12	Innocent, yet died with transgressors.
Psalm 22:16	Hands and feet pierced.
Psalm 22:18	Cast lots for his clothing.
Isaiah 53:3–10	Beaten, mocked, and spat upon.
Psalms 34:20	Died with no broken bones.
Isaiah 53:9	Buried in a rich man's tomb.

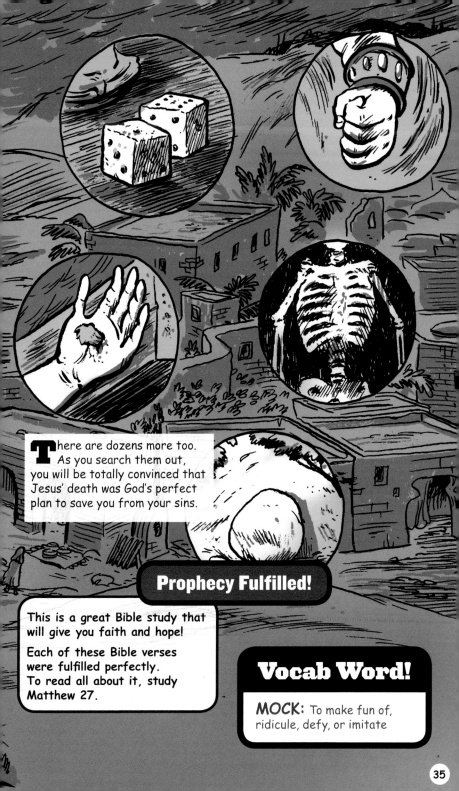

There are dozens more too. As you search them out, you will be totally convinced that Jesus' death was God's perfect plan to save you from your sins.

Prophecy Fulfilled!

This is a great Bible study that will give you faith and hope!

Each of these Bible verses were fulfilled perfectly. To read all about it, study Matthew 27.

Vocab Word!

MOCK: To make fun of, ridicule, defy, or imitate

16 The Temple Is Toppled

The Bible talks about Jesus coming and dying for us, but did you know Jesus Himself was a prophet too?

He made an amazing prediction that happened long after He left the earth!

When? In A.D. 30

The Prophecy

Matthew 24:1, 2

"You see all these, do you not? Truly, I say to you, there will not be left here one stone upon another that will not be thrown down."

Jesus said the Jewish temple in Jerusalem would be destroyed. Some of the stones that made up the temple were 100 tons!

This prophecy was fulfilled in A.D. 70, nearly 40 years after Jesus went back to heaven, when the Romans attacked Jerusalem.

Josephus, a trusted historian, tells us that the Roman invaders even dug up the very foundations of the temple!

Prophecy Fulfilled!

100 TONS

This is another powerful example that Jesus is indeed the Son of God and that you can trust Him with your future.

Vocab Word!

INVADE: To enter forcefully as an enemy; hostile intent

So far, we've looked at a lot of prophecies from a long time ago, but now let's look at some that are being fulfilled today!

Here's an ancient prophecy that we see being fulfilled right now in our time ...

When? In A.D. 50

The Prophecy

2 Timothy 3:2-5

"For men will be lovers of themselves, lovers of money, boasters, proud, blasphemers, disobedient to parents, unthankful, unholy, unloving, unforgiving, slanderers, without self-control, brutal, despisers of good, having a form of godliness but denying its power."

The apostle Paul says that the earth will experience moral decline in the last days.

NEARER, MY GOD, TO THEE...

©⚡#!!

Today, many people—many who say they love Jesus—are addicted to bad things. Bible writers living 2,000 years ago would be shocked at what we do for entertainment!

Too many people today have already fulfilled this prophecy. The Bible says we should "turn away from such people!"

Prophecy Fulfilled!

When we do good things and we're good to each other, Jesus is happy. When we are unloving to each other, or unthankful, or unforgiving, Satan is the one who is happy. You don't want to make him happy, do you?

Vocab Word!

BLASPHEMER: A person with no respect for God, or irreverence to God or sacred things

18 Jesus and the Last Days

Jesus, our Savior and Lord, often spoke about the last days. And since He is the very Son of God, we can trust what He has to say about the future ...

The Prophecy

Read Matthew 24

Jesus said that in the end times, our little world would be filled with big natural disasters—such as earthquakes, tsunamis, and disease—and also wars and violence (Matthew 24). Does it seem like this has come true just as Jesus said?

Jesus also said that after the gospel goes to the whole world, the end will come. Now, that's good news, isn't it? When the end comes, your eternal life will just be starting!

When?
In A.D. 30

40

Prophecy Almost Fulfilled!

Today, with radio, TV, books, DVDs, satellite, the Internet, and missionary work, the gospel is going to the world faster than ever before!

Did you know God's church has representatives in nearly every one of the world's 200 nations and territories?

Yes, Jesus is coming soon to fulfill the most wonderful prophecy of them all!

You can play a big part in Jesus' return. When you give of your time to help your church spread the good news, Jesus is using you to fulfill this prophecy!

Vocab Word!

GOSPEL: The good news of Jesus' forgiveness and His soon return